VISUAL CHORDS

Visual Chords

Poems

Jianqing Zheng

BROKEN TRIBE PRESS

Visual Chords
Copyright © 2025 Jianqing Zheng

First Edition

Paperback ISBN: 978-1-965412-25-1

Cover photograph by Dorothea Lange
Cover art design by Jacob Arms

Published by Broken Tribe Press
Lawrence Landing Company
Raleigh, North Carolina 27609
USA, North America

Broken Tribe Press is a proud member of:

Independent Book Publishers Association
  and
Community of Literary Magazines and Presses

www.brokentribepress.com

CONTENTS

I

II

III

IV

V

I

"The camera is an instrument that teaches people how to see without a camera."

— Dorothea Lange

Lunchtime

—Lunchtime for Cotton Hoers,
Mississippi Delta, June 1937

After hoeing the cotton fields
the whole morning
the girl slumps on the pallet
in a sliver of shade
to gulp a bottle of soda.

Behind her, sunlight spangles
through leaves
like drifting bubbles.

She wears a white bandana
and hoop earrings,
her look a placid pond
with no ripples
in the deep woods.

Soon she stands up,
drags back to work
with other farmhands, ready
to hoe the hot afternoon
into striking bells.

Body Language

—Plantation Overseer and His Field Hands,
Mississippi Delta, 1936

The plantation overseer stands conspicuously,
right foot on the bumper, left arm akimbo,
right hand on the bent knee, and eyes narrowed
into a bossy look behind glasses. His burly

presence overshadows the weary farmhands:
three sitting on the store's stairs, one leaning
against the veranda post, and another poking
his head above the car door. Four of them glance

at the photographer, but the one on the lower
step looks elsewhere, his left hand touching
the chin. Is he looking distracted or gazing
at something more curious than the camera?

In this most southern cotton land on earth,
standing or sitting conveys blues or mirth.

Worn Path

—Ex-Slave with Long Memory, Alabama, 1938

Memory is a worn path
treaded
by
this
old
black
woman
who
holds
a
cane
and
looks
back
at
her
foot
prints

her
eyes
filled
with
long
years
of
hard
ships
which
become
her
strong
will
to wobble forward

Escape

—Homeless Family, Atoka County,
Oklahoma, 16 June 1938

They plod along from place to place looking for a
meager chance of survival, but the unpaved road goes
so long and so rutty across the vast barren land that
there is nothing but the red sunset with open arms in
the distance.

> homeless
> sharing the night
> with stars

Road

—The Road West, U.S. 54 in Southern New Mexico, 1938

The
road
west
goes
so
long
and
so
faraway
with
nowhere
to run
away

Day
after
day
roaming
for
jobs
for
anything
to
keep
them
alive
they
become
the
trodden
road
going
west

Girl by the Fireplace

—Resettled Farm Child from Taos Junction to Bosque
Farms Project, New Mexico, December 1935

When drought turns plains
to dust blown up
into mountains of clouds
to blacken the sky
and bury wherever
they besiege,

the Taos Junction refugees
lose their homeland
and resettle for a new life
on Bosque Farms, but
hunger and poverty
follow like dark shadows.

See, in this dwelling,
a skinny girl sits
on the rustic bench
by the rusty iron bed
with her right hand
supporting her face.

She leans forward,
looking down at the soot-
stained fireplace,
as if contemplating
the essential need
for the warmth of life.

The sun shines in,
pouring some light
on her hair, her back
and the hearth—
a wounded angel
no longer in flight.

Standing Hunger

—White Angel Breadline, San Francisco, 1933

In the breadline outside White Angel,
a soup kitchen established
by Lois Jordan,

a wealthy widow who has fed
more than a million
hungry mouths

in three years, this old man
in an old fedora
stands aloof

from others. He leans pensively
on the wooden fence,
hands clasped,

and circled in his arms
is an empty tin can
waiting to be

filled with soup. What
will tomorrow be?
As depressing

as the lead sky hanging
overhead? Is there
a forecast for it?

A Street Moment

—Man beside Wheelbarrow, San Francisco, 1934

Sitting
    listlessly
    on two

hollow bricks
    against
    the barren wall

with arms
    crisscrossed
    on knees

and head
    lowered
    like a dumbbell

too heavy
    to lift
    from hunger

and despair
    is a man
    wearing

an 8-panel cap
    and worn shoes
    and waiting

desperately
    for a job.
    Beside him

is an overturned
    wheel
    barrow

waiting to be
    turned
    back over.

Endurance

—*A Sign of the Times: Mended Stockings,*
San Francisco, 1934

The neat stitching on the stockings is a sign of
frugality in the Great Depression: the thin lines amaze
our eyes with the presence of a historical pain in
visual grace, and they also show a strong mind of
holding life against the tides of hard times.

gravel road a hard way that leads to life

Mother and Children

—Migrant Mother, Nipomo, California, March 1936

The migrant woman gazes into the distance,
eager to see the shadow of her husband
gone somewhere to have the tools repaired.

Her right hand holds her wrinkled face
as if holding the heavy weight of concerns.
Two girls leaning on her shoulders turn

their backs to the camera, too shy for greetings.
A baby sleeps in her left arm—an image
of Madonna and child. But life isn't a painting,

and migration isn't resurrection when they
crowd under a shabby tent on this pea farm
in the middle of nowhere, trying to find a way.

Cutting

—Filipinos Cutting Lettuce,
Salina, California, June 1935

While the burning sun
snaps its long fire whips
like a grim foreman
sitting astride a horse,
the farmhands bend
their bodies and cut
lettuce row after row.

They cut the sun,
blood-faced, to howl
and fall in pain,
cut evening up
with stars fading in,
and cut weariness
into dream songs.

Responses

—*I Am An American, 13 March 1942*

On December 8, 1941, the day after the surprise attack
on Pearl Harbor, a Japanese grocery owner in Oakland,
California put up a storefront sign: *I Am An American*.
Soon he was forcibly removed to the relocation center.

> summer trip
> to Rohwer Site
> the replica watchtower
> a stern guard
> under the hot sun

Restricted when they arrived by swampy land,
barracks, armed guards, and barbed-wire fences, they
were no longer treated as Americans. Some of them
never leave.

> internees
> laid to rest
> in a strange land
> wandering spirits
> still wondering why

II

Reactions

—Alfred Eisenstaedt's Puppet Show

Parc de Montsouris, Paris. In front of a miniature
stage, children watch a puppet show, their eyes open
wide. When the evil dragon is to be slain, there's a stir
of sound—one girl shrieks a string of "ahhh's,"
another muffles her mouth with small shaking hands,
a big boy stretches his arm shouting "Slay it!" and a
smaller boy stops his ears.

I'm the boy stopping his ears as grandma tells me the
tale of the headless horseman at bedtime. I remember
shivering and pulling the blanket over my face.

> deep autumn
> in front of the shack
> a scarecrow

The Shift of Roles

—Margaret Bourke-White's photographs of women

When World War II dragged men to the battlefields, women became welders, crane operators, oilers, grinders, coil tapers, foundry helpers, and shippers, doing whatever they could and earning the same wages as men. When the War ended, they changed into wives, sisters, mothers, and homebodies. Their roles shifted without notice from their men.

> *It's a boy!*
> the husband utters in joy
> outside the labor room

The Queen and Three Kings

—W. and D. Downey's Four Generations

Queen Victoria was seated, her eyes lowered at little
David sleeping in a lace robe on her lap, while Bertie
and George stood behind her—a four-generation
photograph. Later she wrote to her daughter, who was
Germany's Empress: "It seems that it has never
happened in this country that there should be three
direct Heirs as well as the Sovereign is alive."

> hot noon
> a little boy asks his dad
> for a fried popsicle

Two Stars

—Ruth Harriet Louise's Flesh and the Devil

In *Flesh and the Devil*, Garbo and Gilbert lie on a couch. Her left arm wraps his head like protecting a vase, and he murmurs "Fleka" onto her crimson lips unfurling into two crescent moons. Years later, seeing Gilbert in the street, Garbo uttered to a friend: "Gott, I wonder what I ever saw in him. I guess he was pretty."

> lip-kissing—
> a feel of distance
> from both

Impression

—Arnold Newman's Georges Rouault

The 85-year-old, French Expressionist painter
Georges Rouault sank into a chair while the
photographer, who loved the painter's somber style,
shot stills from different angles. Rouault sat like a still
life, his eyes thinking. After a while, he uttered: "He's
photographed all around me. Does he want to
photograph my derriere?"

> sitting on the porch
> with one leg on the other
> this cornhusk man

Visual Shock

*—Terence Spencer's Two Women Reacting to a
Mannequin Wearing a Topless Evening Dress in a
Store Window on Oxford St.*

Oxford Street, London, 1964. In a shopwindow a
mannequin in a breast-bare dress attracts two women
pedestrians. They can't believe their eyes. Both place
their right hands on their bosoms as if to cover their
shock. Another woman who walks by casts a sidelong
glance at them.

> Getty Museum
> a pause before Rudi Gernreich's
> sumo caftan

Life magazine reported that a London architect's wife
bought an evening dress, topless, and wore it to a
party. All night long a debate of its merits and
demerits continued among partygoers.

> chilly night
> a man holding a cross
> yells on Bourbon Street

Time Off for the Hillbilly Cat

—Ben Mancuso's Elvis Presley at the Warwick Hotel
in New York City

Early January 1957—Elvis is in New York for his third
appearance on "The Ed Sullivan Show." Waiting in the
elevator lobby of the Warwick Hotel, the King of Rock
'n' Roll presses his nose against the mirror as if to avoid
questions from reporters. His face is as brooding as
James Dean's or as placid as a Mississippi bayou.

> first time we see
> Maowang's picture in China
> everyone calls
> his pompadour
> a plane taking off

Is Elvis lost in thought? His eyes fix on nothing, not
even on the poster on the mirror, which jazzes up the
moment with musical notes, clinking glasses, and the
words: *New York Dining at its best in the Celebrity
Cocktail Lounge. Cheers!*

> sudden rain
> drenched in Cat King's songs
> we tap our feet
> to the tape recorder
> and spring thunder

Looking

—*George W. Harris and Martha Ewing's Young Veteran Soldier in Wheelchair on Porch, Walter Reed Hospital, Washington, DC*

The dogwood by the hospital porch begins to lose its foliage after changing its raiment from green to gold and then to flaming red. The leaves, like shards of bloody sunset, drift, glide, and land everywhere on the lawn. Day by day their shine turns dark brown. Stirred by a gust of wind, they scurry rustling ankle-high. Today the bare tree offers another charm: robins, cardinals, blue jays, and mockingbirds leaping, squawking, twittering on the twigs where a few red leaves still dangle.

> five-note birdsong—
> he rolls the wheelchair
> to the window

First Sight

—Grey Villet's Central Park Patrolman

At fish-belly daybreak,
a patrolman walked into

Central Park and was
taken aback by a statue

unveiled the night before:
a naked belly dancer,

like a humanized Venus
coming out of morning bath,

smiled cheerfully at him,
her left arm akimbo,

her right one lifting high
as if to wave "Good morning"

as he strolled past her
pouting and glancing . . .

Monroe's Smile

—*Matty Zimmerman's Marilyn Monroe*
  (The Seven Year Itch)

was a beautiful thing
she kept
for her public image,

something she got to give
as a fireball to burn
gentlemen's hearts,

because some of them
liked it hot, some
preferred blondes, some liked it

as a hometown story
to make love as happy as
ladies of the chorus.

She left it as a heritage
for some to wonder,
imagine or retrospect

when she died at the age of 36—
did she flash out
into LA's city lights,

into sparkling stars over sea, or
into space's constant darkness
where name is nameless,

infinity is endless,
story is storyless, and
smile is a river of no return?

Feeling

—Bob Landry's Kay Kendall & Yul Brynner

In Paris, on the set of
Once More with Feeling,
Kendall and Brynner
fixed a cutout of kiss:
nose touches nose,
so do the chins, while
lips feel for a bridge.

III

"If we can discover the universe in a grain of sand, we can surely parse the American South in a photograph."

— William Ferris

Mississippi Morning

—Horse Pasture

The dewdrops drip
like strands of dreads
from pine trees,

the sun rises
like a cowboy with a bandanna
swinging a lasso of light,

the low fog lingers
like a herd of horses
grazing the rolling pasture,

the white fence zigzags
like a tipsy farmer
in unsteady steps,

somewhere
two cardinals share songs
like soundtrack

to the motion
of this morning's
tranquil moment.

A View from Fisher Ferry Road

—Rose Hill Church Pasture

Three pine trees look like ballerinas on tiptoes about
to pirouette for a premiere show. The shades of blue
are brushing the sky, a perfect backdrop to silhouette
these slender spirits of nature. Mist rises, swaying
long sleeves here and there like backup dancers, and
crickets chirp like low-voice accompaniment. This
serene moment sounds so close, so dreamy, so far
away for the hearing eye. See, the wooden church on
the hill dims into dusk.

> night porch
> a momentary stay
> with stars

Long Standing

—Amanda Gordon, Rose Hill Church

The old woman in her Sunday best
stands on the church porch:
a white dress, a pearl necklace,
a blue handbag in her left hand,
a straw hat adorned with white flowers.

As calm as the land
under the Mississippi sun,
she looks like a weathered totem pole.

Her walking cane,
almost invisible by her dress,
reveals her inner strength:
washing clothes in a tin basin
in front of her shanty
which has resisted falling
in the storms of hard times.

Daily Use

—Homemade Patchwork Quilt by Amanda Gordon

Amanda and four children
unfold a patchwork quilt
before their ramshackle shack:
an enchanting piece of art
sewn with strips of fabric
cut from disused shirts,
pants, sacks, and curtains.

It shows imagination
to beautify the mind,
rivers to irrigate the fields,
voices to vivify the land,
and hardships to glorify life
as plain as this quilt
sewn for daily use.

Patchwork Quilt (Haiku)

—Pecolia Warner with Her "P" Quilt

patchwork quilt
a daily-use folklore
threaded with sunlight

Soulful Dancer

—Unidentified Street Actress

She is expressing herself, her shoulders bouncing,
chest jilting, eyes sparkling with autumn sunshine.
Jerking and stomping, popping and locking, wiggling
and backsliding, she casts her smile to a streetful of
whistles and clapping hands.

> county fair
> a butterfly flutters
> head to head

Road Stop

—S. M. White & Son Crossroads Store

In the deep autumn
the crossroads store looks barren
like its surroundings,

the light bulb inside
is like a constant burning
of a thin matchstick,

on the dusty door
are the two faded signs
of Colonial Food,

on the rustic porch
are the two empty benches
waiting for locals

to sit on for a while
to chat and laugh. There are
more signs on the ground

or nailed on the wall
and columns: Coca-Cola,
Double Cola, and

Orange Crush. They add
a feel of the bygone years.
A Chevron gas pump

in front of the store
has rusted. After grabbing
two shots, I get back.

onto the road which
winds on with no more stops
to see small wonders.

Closed

—Bus Barn

Our mission is to provide
safe and efficient transportation.

If nobody's here please call
638-0377 or 638-7755.

I grab shots of the sign
with my shadow creeping

on the wall, wondering who will
answer the phone when it's closed.

Delta Blues

—One-String Guitar by Louis Dotson

The farmhand sits on the porch
feeling the wind whistle past the fields:
dancing corn dancing corn
dancing corn in wind

The farmhand sits on the porch
hearing the lightning strike across the sky:
bending rice bending rice
bending rice in lightning

The farmhand sits on the porch
seeing the sunshine over the horizon:
blooming cotton blooming cotton
blooming cotton in sunshine

The farmhand sits on the porch
waiting for the evening to befall him:
flat life flat life
flat life of the flatland

The farmhand sits on the porch
playing a self-made diddley bow:
whining blues whining blues
whining blues through night

Delta Heat

—Unidentified Rider and Pony

The street with a few old cars
parked on the roadsides
sizzles under the summer sun.

No one can tolerate the heat.
Then, a rider appears,
sitting astride a small white pony.

He looks smug and heavy
like a policeman on patrol and
his face glitters with sweat.

The hooves clatter
like rhythmical drum grooves
to beat heat into heat again.

Preaching

*—Sanctified Church of God in Christ,
   Clarksdale, Mississippi*

The holy time
to stimulate

exhilaration
one after another

from the congregation
whose claps

and ring shouts
shake loose

themselves
and incite

the wooden church
to join the shake.

After Church

—Clover Valley M.B. Church

Sunlight is slanting through the windows of this small wooden church to add a bluish shade to the brown and gray backs of old pews. On one end of a pew lies a white paddle fan, like a kitten curling up to reclaim the good of silence which sprawls like kudzu in the presence of Holiness.

> waking dream
> the in and out
> of a butterfly

Wheatfield after Spring Rain

—Home on Highway 27, between Utica and
  Crystal Springs, Mississippi

All I wish for
is a lump of soil
to smell the petrichor
of old days that plow
sunrise up and sunset down

Hayfield (Haiku)

—The Hay-Baling Team on Broadacres

golden hayfield
blacks and whites work together
under the blue sky

Long Time No See

—Metal Chairs on Front Porch

Mark and Tiger who haven't seen
each other for fifty years

after they left Mississippi
sit cross-legged in the porch chairs

sharing childhood memories.
Oftentimes after school

they went fishing together
in the Sunflower River.

Once they caught a big catfish, but
it wriggled free from Tiger's hands

after Mark unhooked it.
The two also created a blues duo

performing on the porch
in the evenings. Mark boomed

like Little Milton and Tiger played
a harmonica like Sonny Boy.

They attracted many kids around them
like moths around bright lights.

Many nights they dreamed of
going somewhere, realizing

they couldn't be the hooked fish
struggling desperately out of water.

Mark went up to the Windy City
to sing in a club and Tiger

joined the navy to see the world.
Now they return, recollecting

their old days—gold grains sieved
from the sunset over their dreamland.

The Day of Departure (Tanka)

—Mailboxes, 11188 Fisher Ferry Road

Two red mailboxes
stand side by side by the fence
seeing off the sun
    which waves its golden rays
    as if reluctant to leave

Couple

—Lee Cooper and Joe Cooper, Kent's Alley,
   Leland, Mississippi

Love is molecules
joining atoms
for chemical reactions,

it's plain life
like they hold hands
till old age,

it's oneness
as staunch as their roots
gnarling together

like a Delta blues song
dedicated to
wind and rain,

sun and moon,
and the flatland
underfoot.

No Loitering

—No Loitering Sign, Mississippi Delta

The term painted in white on the earthy red wall of a closed corner store lies like a dead drunk in the shallow standing water on the concrete. No loafer roams around, no car booms past, no trotting dog lolls out its tongue and pees to claim territory. The Delta has its unique quiet and slowness: a liquor sign paling on the other side of the street, a pickup truck napping by the curb, a bayou covered with green scum, a cornfield rustling and browning in fall wind, a red-eared slider staying still on a fallen log, or a man languishing on a porch one late afternoon, but it also has a temper: a windstorm blowing a blues through woods and fields, a tornado flexing its muscles while twisting over small towns and hamlets. Whatever it is, life never loiters here; it plows the flatland into fresh green each spring.

       forgotten churchyard
       frequented by wind
       headstones
       appear to peer
       among high weeds

Reflection on the Lake

—Wes Carter Lake, Warren County, Mississippi

It is a ripple of light and shadow
that deforms something
or nothing in the breeze.

Even the clouds floating leisurely
need a moment to immerse
their white robes in water.

Snapping shots by the lake,
I catch a moment of reflection
on the lake of the mind.

What's visual may not be
what's seen by the mind's eye.
In a sense, existence

is a state of nonexistence,
time is timeless,
and root is rootless.

The reflection on the lake
dims out when the sun dips
into its reflection, into darkness.

Summertime

—Unidentified Watermelon Vendor and Son

The vendor and his son stand
by a white pickup peddling

watermelons, their faces
the shine of the southern sun.

The boy holds a cut melon
and urges me to taste it,

his broad smile an invitation
of the Mississippi heat.

Smiling back, I grab the shot
of this sweet moment.

IV

"Suddenly, I found myself surrounded by sand and shadows which kept changing with every step. It then became a race with the setting sun .... It felt like I was chasing shadows."

— Leo Touchet

Sandscape

—Eureka Valley Sand Dunes #0721

The dunes
      are curving,
            rounding,
                 or slanting
            into magic
      shapes
of shadow
      and light
            to form
                 a live view
            of abstract art:
      a sleeping
beauty
      in stillness
            and motion
                 making you
            utter
      Eureka
upon seeing her.

Questions from Seeing

—Eureka Valley Sand Dunes #0758

The background shadow looks like
a mummy of an Egyptian pharaoh

and the foreground sand ripples like
a pyramid labyrinth in darkness.

If ancient burial means eternal peace,
why should it be disturbed?

But after the buried is unearthed
for research or exhibition, what is seen

after a mummy is unwrapped cautiously?
An object for preservation study or

a body as dry as a dead Joshua tree?
As you walk near a mummy case

in the museum, do you shudder
at those big, painted, and staring eyes?

Who has a stronger desire to see?
A researcher, a museumgoer, or

the dry mummy who may be able
to silently watch us doing whatnot?

A Way of Seeing

—Monahans Sandhills State Park #1110

    Those
        sand
dunes

    (tension
        of time
and space

    touch
        of light
and shadow

    shape
        of solitude
and company)

    look
        serene
and jumpy

    under
        sun
and moon

    as if
        ready
to swing

dance
in swirling
wind

each
a mass
of harmony

and
dissonance
between

being
and
nonbeing

Seeing the Shadows

—Monahans Sandhills State Park Dunes #1734

Now a seagull
drifting on ripples,

now an origami
with folded wings,

now an iceberg
collapsing into sea,

now nothing
but hulking dunes

resembling
burial mounds,

now shadows
changing shapes

with light sliding
across sands—

a long reptile
wriggling into

a silhouette
against seeing.

Jazz Funeral

1. Last Show

—Pallbearers Carrying the Coffin #0010

Wind
swings
down
the
street
to
the
somber
beats
of
jazz

the
casket
swings
too—
the
last
show
of
the
dead
musician

2. Last Bye

—Playing in a Jazz Funeral Procession #0059

The camera

joins
the
dirge

leading the jazz procession to the cemetery

then
the
second line

led by a whining clarinet and drums:

blow
beat
bebop
boom

Cool! The farewell stomps into celebration

3.   The Dance

—The Second Line #0004

Colorful umbrellas
hip
& hop

strut
& booty
bounce

rejoicing
the dead
turning

in the
above ground
tomb

Being in the Moment

—New Orleans #1599

Two lovers form a silhouette
in the halo
of the southern sunset,

heads tilting, eyes smiling,
arms hugging
for a soulful presence.

She's the crescent moon
throbbing
with his heartbeat,

and he Lake Pontchartrain
rocking her
into a mooring boat.

V

Fireflies at Dusk

—Keith Carter's Fireflies

A boy runs to the pond to catch
fireflies glowing off and on
above water. A gray-haired man
fishing on the pier puts down
his rod to watch. When a firefly
drifts by, the boy flings his hand

to catch and put it in the jar
fastened to his waist. It's getting
dark now, and a few stars
start to twinkle. More and more
fireflies blink over the pond.
The old man keeps watching.
Now and then he flings his hand
as if to catch a glow of childhood.

Snowscape

—Cynthia Matthews' Bryant Park

Snow is falling
on Manhattan's skyscrapers,
noise and luxury,

falling into a picture:
two figures
holding black umbrellas

walk through Bryant Park;
their footsteps
on the fallen snow

fade into Manhattan's
stillness, fade into snow
falling in a hush.

Wildwood Chapel

*—Terry Donnelly's Wildwood Chapel under Bigleaf
Maples in Fall Color*

The closed white chapel
is surrounded
by the murmurs of

gold maple leaves
spinning down
with sunlight

to the black roof,
the ground and
the chapel's doorstep.

At this moment
how I wish
the door would open

for the murmurs
to drift in
and whisper

autumn's message
into the quietness
of the chapel.

Into Autumn

—Scott T. Smith's photograph
(creative # 520435852)

Saturday afternoon
while walking on a trail
I see a maple leaf
shining bright red
on the blades
of the long golden grass.

As I walk toward it,
a whiff of wind
blows it up into the air.

Like a red butterfly,
it flutters farther
and alights back
on the shiny blades
of the long golden grass
waving with autumn sunlight.

Bird Play

—Lisa Thornberg's The Unspoiled Beaches at Padre Island National Seashore

A little girl runs to the beach
to chase seagulls
lifting, skimming, thrusting,

soaring over white waves
or drifting overhead
and looking for something

worth pecking. Appearing
in the lens, the girl
and gulls are cooing, squealing,

flapping or float-dancing
for more snapshots
while waves are lapping

like tap-dancing sheep
at this moment of interbeing.

Beside Quiet Waters

—Terry Bidgood's Jamaica

A mooring blue boat
rocking in the lapping
of blue waves
is about to sail to sea.

When faith is a boat
sailing in the vast sea
life has its goal
and meaning.

Retracing Jesus' Steps

*—Terry Bidgood's photographs in The Lands of the
Bible Calendar 2021*

>   page by page
>   each turn
>   into a new view

shepherds' field
sunshine billowing
for the birth of Jesus

>   Nazareth rocks
>   dotted with purple flowers
>   a view of Christ's home

Jordan River
His baptism
a constant flow

>   Judaean Desert
>   Jesus' fasting descends
>   to the Dead Sea

time-worn ruins
of Capernaum synagogue
His voice remains

>   sermon on the mount
>   the groundwork of all lives
>   for all seasons

morning temple
Jesus' steps
steady as rock walls

Dome of the Rock
atop it the Father
looks to the Son

gold-gilded Dome
the sun opens its arms
to the messiah

Passover
in the upper room
Christ's blood in the cup

Garden of Gethsemane
Jesus' loneliness
in each blooming flower

Via Dolorosa
way to the cross
a route of pilgrimage

Holy Sepulchre
sunshine from the dome
the light from Him

garden tomb
Jesus Christ
rising again

boat on the sea
following Him
to new life

Note: "Garden of Gethsemane" is written after Alex
Soh's photograph in the same source.

Smog Angel

—Lintao Zhang's Beijing Is Enveloped in Smog

Her sole duty is
to add shades of gray
to the polluted sky

brushed with
a light touch
of dirty brown.

Birds are gone
from leafless trees,
highrises look like

standing mummies
in burial shrouds,
and cold wind

is a choked sob
for the second coming
of the blue sky.

Four Haiku

—Claudia Brefeld's photographs

1

morning wind
petrichor of earth
refreshes the mind

2

spring (memories crisscross green grass) again

3

meadow breeze
flight of light
off dandelion florets

4

seascape all rocks push and shove to shore

Acknowledgments

Many thanks to the editors of the acknowledged journals, who first published my work, and deep gratitude to William K. Lawrence, Publisher-in-Chief of Broken Tribe Press, and readers for selecting this manuscript.

Arkansas Review: "Long Standing," "Long Time No See," "Mississippi Morning"

Blip Magazine: "The Queen and Three Kings," "Two Stars"

Catalyst: "Hayfield," "Patchwork Quilt"

Contemporary Haibun Online: "No Loitering," "Responses"

Deep South Magazine: "Body Language."

Delta Poetry Review: "Being in the Moment," "Delta Blues," "Seeing the Shadows," "Worn Path"

Digging through the Fat: "Lunchtime"

Haibun Today: "Looking," "Reactions," "Visual Shock"

Haiga in Focus: "Four Haiku" ("meadow breeze," "morning wind," "spring")

Hawaii Pacific Review: "Cutting"

Hummingbird: "Feeling"

Intégrité: "A View from Fisher Ferry Road," "After
　　Church," "Beside Quiet Waters," "Endurance,"
　　"Preaching," "Retracing Jesus' Steps"
I Wanna Be Loved by You: Poems on Marilyn Monroe
　　(anthology): "Monroe's Smile"
Louisiana Literature: "Fireflies at Dusk"
MUSE Literary Journal: "Smog Angel"
Off the Cuffs (anthology): "First Sight"
Poetry South: "Escape," "Girl by the Fireplace,"
　　"Soulful Dancer," "Standing Hunger"
POMPA: "Closed," "Into Autumn," "Road," "Road
　　Stop," "The Day of Departure"
Red River Review: "The Shift of Roles"
Ribbons: Tanka Society of America Journal:
　　"Time Off for the Hillbilly Cat"
Right Hand Pointing: "Wheatfield after Spring Rain"
Rooted Magazine: "Couple," "Reflection on the Lake"
San Pedro River Review: "Delta Heat," "A Street
　　Moment"
Shamrock (Ireland): "Impression"
Still Motion: "A Way of Seeing"
The Kerf: "Snowscape," "Wildwood Chapel"
The Southern Quarterly: "Daily Use"
WCP Magazine: "Questions from Seeing,"
　　"Sandscape"

THE AUTHOR

Jianqing Zheng is the author of *The Dog Years of Reeducation*, *A Way of Looking*, and five poetry chapbooks and e-chapbooks; editor of seven scholarly books, including *Conversations with Dana Gioia* and *Sonia Sanchez's Poetic Spirit through Haiku*; and coeditor of four scholarly books, including *Dana Gioia: Poet & Critic*. He received the 2019 Gerald Cable Book Prize, 2001 Slapering Hol Press Chapbook Award, and three Mississippi Arts Commission poetry fellowships, among other awards and honors. He is a professor of English at Mississippi Valley State University, where he founded and edits the *Journal of Ethnic American Literature* and *Valley Voices: A Literary Review*. Zheng's poems have appeared in numerous magazines and journals, including *Another Chicago Magazine*, *Arkansas Review*, *Birmingham Poetry Review*, *Mississippi Review, Cimarron Review*, *Hanging Loose*, and *Spillway*.